POUR THE WHISKEY OVER MY HEART AND SET IT ON FIRE

~

BOGDAN DRAGOS

Pour the Whiskey Over My Heart and Set It On Fire
Copyright © 2020
HST & Bogdan Dragos

Horror Sleaze Trash
horrorsleazetrash.com

some things can never be put back together

Some things can never
be put back together
after they've been
taken apart

No matter how much
willpower is involved

One of those things,
she now knew for sure,
was a marriage

Like the one
she was presently fleeing,
flying down the highway
like a fiend or a bat out of hell

Another such thing
could be her right hand
resting severed on the seat
there beside her

Though she wasn't so
sure about the hand
Maybe if she made it
to the hospital in time?

Maybe

don't get in grandpa's way

When grandpa gets drunk
don't get in his way

Just don't

He'll not seek trouble with anyone
living though
Oh no, he'll go grab his shovel
and go into the backyard
and start digging

and cursing

digging and cursing

He'll be digging after the body
of his dead brother
who once cheated him
out of a business
and a potential marriage

He gets so carried away with this
that once an innocent puppy
was decapitated
by the blade of his shovel

Don't get in grandpa's way
when he's drunk

Just don't

cartoonist

Dad was fat all his life
Obese
He couldn't do a lot of things
Walk without special help
Bathe
Climb stairs
Sit in a normal chair
Drive a normal car
Sleep in a normal bed
And say "I love you, son."

To draw those words out
of his dad he became a cartoonist,
but that also failed

And now that his father
was dead,
collapsed face down
on the kitchen floor,
blood seeping out
of a head wound,
he struggled to turn him over,
roll him on his back
and he dipped his finger in the blood
and drew a speech bubble
next to his father's head
and wrote in it those unspoken words

Finally:
"I love you too, dad."

what's a chlamydia, dad?

There are a few advantages
in having a blind daughter

For one
she can't see you
when you beat your wife

He covered her mouth
with his hand and started
punching at her randomly

"Oh dear, I love you
so much," he said
for the blind girl to hear
"I appreciate you immensely
for sneaking out of the house
several nights in a row, leaving
our angel of a daughter alone,
while I was at work,
so you could go and get
the most wonderful gift
for my birthday.
Oh dear, I absolutely love
this chlamydia you gave me.
Thank you, dear.
Thank you so much!"

bachelorette party

The driver:
He's got the best chance
at survival in a car crash

That's why he made it
and the other three didn't

Having the seat belt on
also helped immensely

Knowing that the accident
would happen was also
a plus

Yep, the only minus of the situation
was having to pretend
he had PTSD and depression
and whatnot
for causing the deaths
of three close friends

who'd talked his fiance
into a gangbang
the night before

proposal

"Look, boy," the nurse told him
"To the extent you're not ashamed
of your own underwear
to see your private parts,
to that extent you should not
be ashamed of me, okay?"

He looked at her
with a smirk
shrugged

"Thing is," said the nurse,
"a lot of people who use sex toys
are not doing it the right way.
If you ask me, they should
truly advertise this shit on TV.
Don't buy your phallic toys
without a flat base.
Your anus, you see,
is like a vacuum,
it will suck things in
once they pass a certain point.
And believe me, you don't
want that to happen.
Things stuck up one's butt
are the norm in here.
I'm used to them.
But, with you I see
it's in the urethra.
You stuck something
up your dick hole.

There are some who do so.
And they get quite creative
with their explanations.
Who would've thought
fear of embarrassment
gives people such godlike creativity?
But most are not very creative.
The other day, a kid tried
to convince us that the strings
found in his urethra
were from his underwear.
It's just underwear fluff
lodged in my dick hole, he said.
Bull-fucking-shit, pal.
You don't need to lie here.
It just makes our job
a thousand times harder.
So... What's your story
then, mister?"

"You pull things out of people's
bodies for a living, right?" he asked

"Uh, yes, that I do..."

"Great, then could you please pull this out?"
He pointed at his erect penis
and the thin wire thingy
sticking out of it

"Not gonna tell me
how it got there?" she asked
"You're no fun."

"I'll tell you afterwards," he said

"It's a deal," she said,
grabbing her tweezers,
pinching them around
the wire as she pulled

It had something attached to it,
something dragging behind,
something like a very long label,
like a fortune cookie note
and it said:

MARRY ME?

"WHAT. THE. FUCK."
she said, staring up
into his eyes

He just smiled back down
at her and winked

Two years later...
they were both still single

134

"The angriest I ever got," she said,
"Was with an ex-boyfriend, of course.
I just wanted him to die.
But like, not casual wanting him to die.
Really, really wishing with all my might
that he'd drop dead.
I felt I couldn't go on living
as long as I knew he was alive.
I had to do something about it.
I was literally about to explode.
So, to prevent that, I got dressed
and despite the rain and all
I went straight to the nearest pet shop.
Bought me a hamster.
And with a red marker,
I wrote my boyfriend's name
on its back.
And then slammed that hamster
against the wall134 times.
For the 134 hours we'd been together.
I calmed down after that.
But, you know,
I don't like talking
about myself all that much.
Tell me about yourself.
Also, what should we get
from the menu?
Have you decided yet?"

seeking God's word

He put a grain of salt
into his right ear
to hear the voice
of God

It didn't work

And he said,
"Must be because
of the grain of pepper
I have in my left year.
The devil's voice
cancels out God's."

And he scooped around
into his left ear
trying to get
the pepper grain out

He used a toothpick
a spoon
a knife
a needle

Nothing worked
and the ear was bleeding
profusely
and it pained him
a great deal

And he passed out

At the hospital
they told him
that his method
for seeking the words
of God is obsolete
and people
hadn't practiced it
for hundreds of years

Today there was
medicine for that
and they gave
him some

He took it
and was now waiting
So far God hadn't said anything
but that was all right
He was feeling
blissfully calm

Maybe silence is
the word of God

There's nothing more soothing
than silence

taking risks

You're not gonna get
anywhere in life
without taking risks
now and then

Yes, father was right

These days he thought
a lot about
his father's words

Not gonna get anywhere in life
without taking risks

Sure

Father took a risk
when he divorced mother
and remarried this other
younger woman

Risks

Risks

Keep on risking

He rolled over in bed
and pinched her
naked breast
squeezing around the nipple

"What are you doing?"
she asked, waking up

"Nothing, dear stepmother.
Just checking if I was taking
the right risks or not."

to become a man

A boy's duty is to become a man
Everything else is a failure
He heard the famous words
more than twenty times a day

The words haunted him
even his dreams

And he was only ten

Father's word was law
And the law said
he had to become a man
because he was born a boy
It was his God-given duty
To become anything else
was to become a failure

The very day he turned ten
his gift was a trip to the forest
Cold place
He didn't understand at first
why the puppy he'd got as a gift
from his mother
had to come along

But it was soon made clear

Father tied the puppy to a tree
and sprinkled him with canned fish

Climbing up into the tree stand
father put a gun in his hands
"If you wanna see your pet live,
save him. Shoot all the predators
drawn to him from now until sunset."

But as luck had it
no predators showed up
and sunset was drawing near

The puppy kept crying
tied to the tree
hungry
cold
afraid

It was calling to him
with almost human words
and it was saying that
there was a shortcut

There is a shortcut
to becoming a man
it seemed

Yes

He turned around and pulled the trigger

BANG!

Hands on his chest,
the old man fell to his knees
And when their eyes were level
he flashed the brightest,
most warming smile
of all his life

lifeguard

Who would've thought
that a job based on saving
people's lives would pay
so ridiculously low?

Life's a beach
for these people,
the lifeguards

But he kept telling himself
he wasn't in it for the money
Oh, no, he would get plenty
of that after he married
the love of his life

Until then,
she would pretend she's drowning
and needs CPR so he could
save her again and again
and put his lips over hers
and thrust his tongue
in her mouth and all that

It's hard to do the kissing thing
and all when your girlfriend's
not yet eighteen so the excuse
to get physical with her
has to be hella good

He judged his as adequate
The show would only have to go on
for another few more months or so

allergies

"Are you trying to kill me?"
his mother screamed
"Are you trying to
fucking kill me!?"

He backed away.
"Mom, please..."

"Shut up! You brought a cat.
A cat! Of all things. In the house!
Knowing full well of my allergies.
THAT is a declaration,
young man.
A declaration that speaks
very loudly.
You are trying to kill
your own mother,
you insane monster!"

An hour later
he was in his room
caressing the cat's head
and back
while it lay purring
on his chest

"Can you believe her?"
he said to the cat

"Hardly," said the cat
"She was the monster, though.
You made the right choice, baby."

"When I decided to keep you?"
he asked

"Yes," said the cat
"And when you stabbed her
in the chest thirty times.
You're such a good boy.
That's why I love you.
And after I help you
calm down you can
drag her body down
to the basement.
I'll consume a bit every day
until there's nothing left
but bones and some guts
you can flush down the toilet."

"I love you too," he said

the thing before the thing before the thing

Because it's nice to be young
because it's nice to be in
your early to mid twenties
and it's nice to do the thing
after you've done the thing

The thing that comes
after you've done the thing
is always the same but
the thing that leads to the thing
is often different

That night it was white powder
they shared it neatly
between each other
then climbed into bed

"Christ," he said "I still can't believe
you sucked dick for this shit.
And a whole carload of it.
What was it, like four, five guys?"

"Oh, shut your hole, you pauper-ass.
If you had a job like a decent motherfucker,
I wouldn't have to do that shit, you know?"

"Shit, baby, don't make this
trip worse than it already is…"

"You started it."

"Whatever, let's just get to the next thing
already."

"I haven't even bathed. You know,
after taking on those guys…"

But it was too late to think

The first thing kicked in,
hard
and it lead to the other thing
and a brain wasn't needed
for either of them

And a cold wind blew in
through the broken window
and dried up their salty sweat

real men

She told me that women
like men with grizzled,
bestial faces, men with scars
men with eyepatches,
men with very unkempt beards
Mouths that snarl
when it's time to smile
Eyes that are like eggs
buried in a nest of wrinkles
Noses that are never straight
And the jaw,
oh the jaw has to be big,
square,
like a chest of drawers
A man's face must have a chin
that can take sledgehammers

That's why the luckiest woman
in the whole wide world
had been Belle
from The Beauty and The Beast
That was a real man, The Beast
although the story is a tragic one
because in the end he turns
into a charming prince
with a smooth face and
fine polished features

"What a fuckboy," she said
"If only he stayed a beast..."

Meanwhile I think about myself
The most grizzly feature
about my face is the mad
eyestrain I developed
because of my job,
staring at monitors in a dark room
for all those years before
coming home to stare at another
Now it is impossible
for me to get outside
and keep my eyes open
like a normal person
I die if I don't strain them
as hard as I can
Sunglasses don't even help
and there's also the dark
circles below my eyes

"They have the texture
of the skin around an asshole,"
she said, laughing

She wasn't wrong

She was also right
when she pointed out
that if you can't grow a beard
by the time you're twenty
you'll never grow
a proper beard

"Shit," I said
"Guess I'll never
be a beast."

"It's never too late
to get your face fucked up
though," she said
"You just need to
start hanging around
the right kind of people."

"Such as your dad?" I asked

"Oh fuck you," she said,
dragging the blanket
up over her breasts

Golden Tongue

In the village
they nicknamed him
Golden Tongue

Because
of course
he had the gift of speech
and would inspire and motivate
all who would listen
Almost like a cult leader

But he never sold
anyone anything
He was just a great speaker
He spoke for God
and helped so many sinners
return to the right path

But of course
as time passes
the meaning of words
tends to shift

Today
no sinner sought to be saved
by Golden Tongue

Just a bunch of giggling girls
who were always seeking him
for some reason

Cyst

You ever just sit or lay on your bed
and stare at the ceiling and wonder
if you've ever eaten meat from an animal
that was the offspring of another animal
you've eaten?

I'd once read an article
about the industry's secret glue
pasting together bits of meat
from many different animals
as if they were all from one

Thus you could eat beef
thinking it's from a single cow
when in fact it's from nine different cows
of nine different ages and breeds

A friend of mine declared herself vegan
after she sliced into a steak and found
slimy gray puss oozing from within it

"I'm a vegan forever from now on!"
she screamed at the sight
of the cyst

And I said, "I'm a writer."

"What?" she asked
"What's that have to do
with what I just said?"

"I'm a writer," I repeated for her benefit
"Meaning I have to compare everything to writing.
Your discovery of the cyst inside the steak
is akin to reading a really nice book
only to reach the most disturbing scene
you've ever stumbled upon
and be taken by surprise
and change your opinion
about the whole entire book.
There are some books like that.
Doesn't mean they all are though.
And unlike a meat eater,
I like to believe that a writer
can tell the difference between a book
written by a single person
and a collaborative project."

"Boy, you're scaring me."

"Can I have that steak?" I asked

"Wah? You... don't mean to eat it, do you?"

"Nah, my cousin has a dog
who surely won't mind the cyst."

She gave me the steak
and she didn't ask,
but the writer equivalent
of this situation would be
to recognize when a story fails
horribly and instead of stubbornly
striving to submit it to agents
you just give it away for free,
publish online, maybe even
under a pseudonym

Anyway, the dog
loved that steak

a girl with a blog

She kept texting me links
links
links
to posts on her blog,
Law of Attraction

Find Your Soulmate In Six
Easy Steps

Meditations For Prosperity

Meditations For Prosperity
Enhanced Edition

14 Visualization Techniques That Will
Manifest The Perfect Life

How To Show Gratitude To The Universe
In Order To Get More Of What You Want

Find Your Dream Job Using This
3-Step Meditation Formula
Works 100%

Grab God's Hand And Let It Pull
You Out Of Debt: Here's How

How To Listen To The Correct
Inner Voice And Let It Guide You

How To Befriend And Make Love To
Your Higher Self: A Step-By-Step Guide

"Leave me a like. Comment too.
Thanks."

"I need an account to do that," I said
"I don't have an account."

"Well, make one."

"I need an e-mail address
to make an account."

"Are you telling me you don't
have an e-mail address?"

"I forgot the password."

"Oh, why do you have to be like that?
You wouldn't move a finger
to help anyone. Ever! How can you
live like that? You're... uhh, horrible!"

"Okay, listen. Here's what I'll do. I'll make
an e-mail address and give you the password
so you can make an account for me
and leave likes and comments
on every post. How about that?"

She didn't answer

And didn't text me for a while after that

A few months later she sent me
an invitation to her wedding

I didn't go

After she got married
she stopped posting on her blog
Her husband was ten years older than her
and they moved to the UK

A few months later a common friend
mentioned she was having a baby
and showed me pictures of it
on the various social media sites
portraying life at its absolute perfection

The account was full of pictures
of quotes from self-help books

'It's never too late to be what
you might have been.'

'Dream positive or wake up!'

'Shoot for the moon! Even if you miss,
you'll still land among the stars.'

'When things aren't going well in your life
scream to yourself STOP and think
of all the ways things can go right
from then on.'

'Remember that what you think
and feel now creates your future!'

'Doing it badly is infinity times
better than not doing it at all.'

'HOPE is the best medicine.'

'Always ask yourself, what would
the best version of myself do?'

'Actions first, feelings later.
Act on your values.'

And on and on
and on

And a few months later
she divorced and returned home
Her girlfriends said the husband
was abusive
The girls who weren't so close to her
said that she cheated on him

The truth was probably
somewhere in the middle

Now she was living on child support
and returned to writing her blog
Only this time the posts weren't so much
about the law of attraction and more
about her life and what she'd been through
and what do you know,
they were actually good
and worth reading

It worked!

The law of attraction had worked

Her blog was finally popular
it was getting likes
and comments and followers
from all around

I read the latest post titled:

When You're Going Through Hell, Keep Going

And it was good
There was some real feeling
behind each line
each word

She'd made it

And now I sit back
waiting for the next post titled:

Nothing Comes Without a Price

Or something like that

testosterone

She doesn't let me drink
and insists
that I listen to her

Insists with
a viciousness

"It's because you work night shifts,"
she says

"What's that got to do with drinking
while I'm free?"

"Alcohol lowers a man's testosterone
and increases his estrogen.
Why don't you know that?
You need to take better care
of yourself."

She made for me a diet
of mostly rice and garlic

Calls me while at work
and tells me to go into the bathroom
and jump 100 times
and do stretching exercises,
Tells me to drink more water
She even buys me bags of nuts and seeds
and tells me to eat them between meals

"No sugar," she says "No, not even
in coffee. Pure black or nothing."

She even bought me a hand grip
strengthener with adjustable resistance
to use while I'm in the office

She encouraged me to eat
raw eggs but stopped when I told her
that you can get salmonella like that

When I came home from work
one evening at 23:36
I ate my rice with garlic
and she asked if I wanted anything else
and I said "Yeah, a beer."

"Okay," she said
Went into the kitchen came back
fifteen minutes later with a cup
of tea and a lemon

"What's this?" I asked

"Ginger tea. It's better with lemon.
Should I squeeze it for you?"

"No thanks, I'll do it myself."
I cut the lemon in half
and squeezed it into the cup

It was the nectar of gods
and I didn't hesitate
to tell her so

"All right then," she said
"Drink it all, rinse with water
before brushing your teeth
and then come to bed."

I did all that
and went to bed
as instructed

And she wanted me to sleep
because lack of sleep
is the worst enemy of a man's
testosterone levels

feeble door

Such a feeble door
It was a joke,
like it was made of cardboard
or something

Permanently ajar, its knob
was barely hanging on
It didn't actually work
and there was no locking it either

There was only one thing
that could ever make it close:
Its gross misalignment
with its own frame
It just kinda stuck that way

It was bad

And it was worse
when daddy got real drunk
and started banging on things
around the house

And it was the worst
when daddy's friends
got him even drunker
made him pass out on the couch
and then came in to play
with his little girl

Tonight would be
one of those times

you cannot kill a poet

Young people,
they think nobody
has the same thoughts as them
They take great pride
in some made up originality

As if really nobody ever thought up
scenarios of themselves descending
some rope from some helicopter
and dropping in the middle of enemy forces
shooting all around all movie like and shit,
and killing all the bad guys
without ever taking a single bullet
A one-man army

Or there's those other thoughts
of simply being the greatest
at some sport and being admired
and envied for your talents

Also, the thoughts of sex in all its forms

The thoughts of mindless violence

Of saving the day

Of being somewhere else
and doing something else

All kinds of thoughts
and all the minds who think them
often consider these original

But they're not
original at all

They're every young person's
dumb-ass thoughts

And me,
I also have thoughts
I consider to be original

I think of how it is to be old
pretty much every damn day
I think of myself being old
and gray and tired and weak
just waiting for death

It's not a very pleasant thought
especially for someone in their twenties
but it's just my way of labeling
my own thoughts as original

Maybe in some wheel chair
nurse pushing me along
No kids
No family
No fortune
No achievements
A life utterly wasted
Death looking down mockingly
and myself looking up at Death
smiling

Motherfucker, you think you got me
but little do you know
that while I was able,
while I was more lively
than a rotting carrot
I defied you by ripping up
tiny little pieces of me
that will stick to the world
long after I'm gone

Oh, they might not be great pieces
or even very good ones
but behind they remain
as you take me away

And ll of them stamped
with my name
It is through them
that I become immortal

And there's nothing
you can do about it

Great, good or bad,
you cannot kill a poet

misbehaving

As felines will hunt
because they are felines
So will children misbehave
because they are children
It's in their DNA
and it's not the exception,
it's the rule

She didn't think it was such a big deal
blasting her music at high volume
and jumping on her bed
in only socks, panties,
and a tank top

But apparently to step-daddy
it was a big deal
for he burst into her room
and announced very loudly
"Listen, if you don't cut that shit
and clean this place up in five minutes
I swear I'll come back
and fuck your ass."

Well surely it was due
to the very loud music
why her ears did not register
the word "up" after "fuck"
in his threat

She just grinned and
turned the music back on
This time a little bit louder

soiled mattress

He sucked in all that smoke,
coughed up a bit

He was lying on the wet,
soiled side of the mattress

It felt warm now

He'd moved it away from the window
ever since that night he broke it
and he'd put up some cardboard
in the frame

He missed the light

"You know," he said,
finally exhaling his plume
"I never did get over
my phobia of skeletons.
Don't quite know how I got it.
Of course it began as a fear.
And then one day my brother
informed me there's one
inside all of us.
We are all skeletons insi..."
He trailed into coughing
Hacked up some phlegm
onto the floor

"Eh, but the smoking
keeps me sane, man.
It doesn't lie to me,
doesn't tell me there's no skeletons.
Nah, that'd be bullshit.
It just helps me to accept the truth.
That's all. And I do.
I accept the truth.
Anyway, what's your fear, man?
And how do you deal with it?"

The man didn't answer
Lying there in silence
slowly soiling his mattress
as before

you both look around and kinda steal stories

I've been accused of many things
in my life but never of being
like a preacher

That is,
until I met her

"There ain't much difference
between you and the preacher
at church," she said

I should've just asked why
but not being very sober
instead I chose to ask her,
"Fucking how?"

She just shrugged

"You both look around
and kinda steal stories,"
she said "If you're out one day
and you see a man jump from a building,
you write about it in your shitty little poems
just like the preacher in his next sermon.
And neither of you will tell the story
exactly how it happened.
You'll both tell it in your own
biased ways."

At this nonsense,
it was my turn to shrug

"You'll grow up one day
and realize so does the news,
so does your parents
and everyone else.
Until then,
why don't we go out
for a change, eh?"

"Sure.
If you'll come with me
to church next Sunday."

Her smile alone
would've been worth it
But, well,
it never happened

sleep paralysis

If a man hits you,
you hit him back
If a kid hits you,
you teach them it's wrong
If a woman hits you,
you just walk away
If a dog bites you, well,
there's no way but to kick it
And if an ant bites you,
you crush it under your thumb

There are ways
of fighting everything

But how do you fight
against a demon?

He found himself asking this
question yet again
He was no possessed man
but sick he definitely was
He sure had a problem, alright

A demon kept visiting him
from time to time
when he fell asleep
And it was no dream
It was sleep paralysis
while he slept
on his back
and it was horrible

"I go to sleep on my side,"
he told the therapist. "Always.
But what can I do, I turn in my sleep and...
well, somehow I end up on my back,
and that's when...
Ah, I know she's not real
and all that, but..."

"Wait. Did you say she?
The demon is a female?"

"Well, yes. She's got large breasts
and long hair cascading over her dress..."

"Aha... Listen, this might sound
a bit avant-garde, but...
I just might have a cure for it.
Here's what you'll have to do,
or rather not do..."

Day fourteen without masturbation
Later evening

He was ready to fall asleep
and his balls felt heavy,
like they could just burst
if he squeezed them hard
enough between his thighs

"Very well then," he told himself
as he placed the drawings
of her under his pillow
"Let her come now."

**I never followed the 'don't keep loser friends'
advice and I don't regret it**

He was always late to the party
Not that this was a party
We just gathered around
to drink and talk about how fucked up
life is and how much
some can fail at it

It's a guys thing

He comes by the time
the beer is running low
and gets himself a can
and sits down

His mouth is red
around the lips
like he didn't wipe the sauce off
after eating spaghetti or something

Not even a full minute passes
before he drops the question
"Yo, can I crush on your couch
for tonight? My girl kicked me out.
Kinda."

"The fuck did you do this time?"

"Oh, not much.
Well, I did lose the job
that her father got me,
just like she said I would.

But that's
besides the point, man.
Really, she got mad at me
cuz early this morning
I got her to sit on my face
and went all in up that pussy.
And then I just notice it's dripping
blood on my face, in my mouth.
What the fuck? I say.
I threw her off and told her
she'd started her period
but turned out I actually cut her
with my tongue piercing.
I took it out right away.
It's still at her place
now that I think about it.
Anyway, we had a fight
and that's that. It'll be over
in a few days. So, do I got
the couch for tonight?
Please?"

We looked at each other
put some money on the table
and sent him to the non-stop
to buy some more beer

**something like a motorbike scratching the asphalt
on the highway**

Her bed was in the corner
of the room
by the window

He watched her
in his mind calling her the girl
who never talks to anyone

She was drawing
Always
with a blue ballpoint pen
on a yellow pad

She'd filled dozens of pages
and had very few left

'And what if they're all
drawings of me?' he thought
'Could be. Not like anyone's
ever seen them."

She drew on
and he watched
and pretended not to

There were screams
and moans and pain-fueled curses
coming from the other rooms
The wheels of stretchers
creaking up and down
the halls

IVs
bandages
blood
needles
and a general rage
against no-smoking rules

But in here, in their room,
all was quiet
except for the sound
of her pen scratching paper

It was like music

Something to fall asleep to:

scratch
scratch

scratch

How soothing
he thought,
almost forgetting
he had no legs
under his blanket

as Rex sat watching through the window

Sitting at the table
with tears in their eyes

The can there between them
Empty bowls before them
a fork laid beside each bowl

He wiped his damp face
and reached for the can,
the opener in his other hand

"No," she said
"I just can't do this.
If not for my dignity,
than at least for poor Rex.
He's the best thing
we've got in our lives.
We can't just eat his food
and let him starve
to death."

He opened the can
and shared its contents,
pouring half in each bowl

"Dogs will find food
outside the house.
It's only in their nature."

"But Rex is a house dog."

"Still a dog, though."

They ate and they cried
and their sleeves grew wet
from wiping their snot
and tears

"I hate you," she said

"I know," he said

And they finished
the whole can
between them

"Mother was right," she said
"That's what I get
for marrying a writer.
I get to eat dog food now."

"I'm sorry..."

It was all he could say

He stood and wiped his mouth
with the back of his hand
and left to go back to work

He was writing a story
about a writer so poor
that his family had to eat
their dog's food

I'd rather not be at this party in the first place

Me
I'd rather dance than make conversation
I'd rather drink than dance
I'd rather not be at this party
in the first place

But I'm looking out the window
glass in hand
and I see you in the yard
under the lamp post
Sitting down in the grass,
plucking at the blades
at your sides

And I wonder
are you like myself?
Do you also wish you weren't
at this party in the first place?
Did you see your boyfriend
making out with another girl?
Or are you just drunk
and a little sick?

You look very pretty
from where I'm watching you

And to think that there's someone
like me at this party
makes me feel kind of…
confused

I pray to God that you're someone
kind of like myself

And then I smile
and walk away from the window
and leave you all alone out there
It's what you truly want
if you're truly like myself
And I guess if other people
can't provide what we want
at least we can give it to each other

I drain my glass
pour another
make a trip to the bar
to ask for ice cubes
Return to the table
and keep drinking

Later I go to the bathroom
and when I come out
I exit through the front door
and slowly walk over
to the spot where you'd sat

You are gone by now
of course
and all that's left behind
is a small patch of red
stained grass

You probably went home
This place wasn't for you
I like you even more for this
I hope you get to be alone
as often as you wish

If you're truly like me
you know how damn
hard that can be

like in the old cartoons, remember?

He drained a pint of beer
and stared down at his belly
feeling it all over

"What are you expecting to happen?"
I asked

He lifted his shirt,
revealing bandages,
then he pointed
in three separate places

"One, two, three.
Stab wounds, bro."

"Stab wounds..?"

"Yep. So I'm expecting the beer
to flow out through them,
just like in the old cartoons,
remember?"

"Um, I don't think that's how
it works in real life, man.
But still, how did it happen?"

"What do you mean
that's not how it works?
If the beer got in my belly,
and there's three holes in my belly,
then why wouldn't it come flowing out?"

I just stared at him
in disbelief

"Man... how much
have you had to drink?"

"It's my first beer. Why?"

"Oh, forget it. Just tell me how it happened,
if you will. Who stabbed you and why?"

"My sister stabbed me.
Three times,
while we were sitting
eating dinner at the table."

"What? Did you touch her
inappropriately again?
Like when you were kids?"

"What? Dude! No!
What the hell do you think I am?
I didn't touch her.
We just had a disagreement,
an argument."

"About what?"

"Well, it's complicated.
My sister's really into politics,
and somehow we reached the topic of abortion.
She disagreed with me, and, well..."

I could only shake my head
in wonder

"Man, you never learn, do you?"

"And now what?" he said

"What?" I said

"Well, aren't you gonna ask me
which side of the abortion issue
I was on?"

"Nope."

"Really?"

"How about another beer?"

"Damn, all right, thanks."

entertainment will be the end of us all

Well
what else to do?

We sit in bed
next to each other
and sweat doing nothing

I take off my shirt
and she says no,
it's not the time

And I tell her to relax
I'm just very hot

Her gaze darts to the screen of my phone
Why? Were you looking at porn?

No, I mean literally
I'm hot because
it's very hot in here

Aha,
and now she laughs
and pretends she was just pulling my leg
with that accusation

But I know she wasn't
She meant what she said

But we don't get to talk about it
because we're both too busy
playing with our phones

And I'm thinking
how others before us,
our parents for example,
must've gotten through such episodes
when the distractions
and the entertainments
were nothing like today

Perhaps they would do the thing
despite the hot weather
and perhaps
we came into the world
because they did the thing
despite the hot weather
Because there were no phones
that could access the internet
at the time
and there was not
much else to do

It was the butterfly effect
at work
I guess

Just like that
two bored people did the thing
because there was nothing
else do to
and their doing of the thing
lead to children who grew up
to invent other things
to be done instead
of doing the thing

Shit, I thought

Humanity is doomed

And it's no nuclear war
no deadly virus
no calamity
no supernova
that will ultimately
do us in

Entertainment will be the end
of us all

9 cubes and 13 glasses

Well there was this night
which had followed a day
An entire day of bad decisions

I remembered that my girlfriend
had put cola in the ice tray
and by now the cubes
must have been ready

I took them out
and placed them one by one
into my glass of whiskey

One cube for one memory
only the very most worst ones

Nine cubes and thirteen glasses
I think went a bit too far

As I sat back in my chair
I prayed up to God
asking if I could
make a living
writing poetry

Ever since that night
I keep hearing what
sounds like laughter
in my ear

I'm still not sure
what it means

to the sunny beach

There always is
and will always be
someone out there
who will miss you

The words that annoyed
him the most
in this world

They rang so
pretentious
in his ears

Of course, only people
who lived nice lives
ever uttered them

The others are those
who don´t wanna
hear such crap

He didn´t wanna
hear such crap
any longer either

So, he undressed himself
and crawled into
the tub

Placed a plank across it
and positioned the toaster
upon on it

He read somewhere online
that it's five times more effective
if you dump a pack of salt
into the water

So he dumped in three

It felt like sand
in the tub
underneath him

He was going
to the sunny beach
Where no one
could ever hurt
him anymore

fade away

FADE AWAY

Why was there a poster in his room
that said FADE AWAY?

It's been around
since like forever
now that he thought about it

And until today
there was no reason
to even think about it
Life was happening fast

It happened so fast
that it's been 52 years
since the day he was born

Today there was nothing left to do
but observe the poster
that said FADE AWAY

And there was nothing else to do
not because he'd done it all
but because he hadn't done shit

52 years and nothing done
Nothing worthwhile anyway

But values change, man
Oh, how they change

One day you're young
thinking failure and shame
and ridicule are what suck

Well, you're not wrong

But

Later when you're old
you realize nothing sucks more
than never risking these things
when you were young

Now this

So now you either tell yourself
that it is never too late to be
what you might've been

Or you sit alone
in your silent room
with no wife
no kids
no pets
and a pension
that comes once a month

And slowly blink your eyes
at your poster that says
FADE AWAY